Civil Liabilities

of New York State Law Enforcement Officers

John J. Sullivan, J.D.

Revised & Maintained by

Lt. Michael D. Ranalli

Looseleaf Law Publications, Inc.

43-08 162nd Street
Flushing, NY 11358
www.LooseleafLaw.com
800-647-5547

This publication is not intended to replace nor be a substitute for any official procedural material issued by your agency of employment nor other official source. Looseleaf Law Publications, Inc., the author and any associated advisors have made all possible efforts to ensure the accuracy and thoroughness of the information provided herein but accept no liability whatsoever for injury, legal action or other adverse results following the application or adoption of the information contained in this book.

©2006 by Looseleaf Law Publications, Inc. All rights reserved. No part of this book may be reproduced, stored in a retrieval system, or transcribed, in any form or by any means, electronic, mechanical, photocopying, recording, or otherwise, without the prior written permission of the Copyright owner. For such permission, contact Looseleaf Law Publications, Inc., 43-08 162nd Street, Flushing, NY 11358, (800) 647-5547, www.LooseleafLaw.com.

Library of Congress Cataloging-in-Publication Data

Sullivan, John J., J. D.
  Liabilities of New York State law enforcement officers/ by John J. Sullivan ; updated and maintained by Michael D. Ranalli.-- 1st ed.
    p. cm.
  Includes bibliographical references and index.
  ISBN 1-932777-07-5
  1. Tort liability of police--New York (State)--Miscellanea. 2. Police misconduct--Law and legislation--New York (State)--Miscellanea. I. Ranalli, Michael D. II. Title.
  KFN5332.6.S85 2006
  345.747'052--dc22
                                                        2005029444

Cover design by *Sans Serif, Inc.* Saline, Michigan

©2006 Looseleaf Law Publications, Inc.
All Rights Reserved. Printed in U.S.A.

Table of Contents

Introduction i

About the Authors iii

Part I - DEFINITIONS 1
   What is a TORT? 1
   What is NEGLIGENCE? 1
   What are DAMAGES? 2
   What does INDEMNIFICATION mean? 2
   What does RESPONDEAT SUPERIOR mean? 2

Part II - CIVIL LIABILITY UNDER NEW YORK LAW 3
   What are some of the consequences to an officer for wrongful conduct? 3
   What are some of the liability issues concerning the operation of MOTOR VEHICLES? 4
   What consideration should be given to the establishment of a roadblock? 6
   What standards govern the USE OF FORCE by the police? 6
   Does Article 35 of the Penal Law set the standards in a civil case concerning the use of force? 7
   What is the case of *Tennessee v. Garner*, referred to in the previous question? 8
   What are some of the INTENTIONAL TORTS that involve police action? 10
   Malicious Prosecution 12
   Are law enforcement officers or their agencies liable for failure to protect an individual? 13
   Are officers liable to injured third parties for failure to arrest intoxicated drivers? 19
   What are the laws relating to indemnification? 20
   Is an officer indemnified if he/she takes police action while OFF-DUTY? 22
   What are the provisions of GML 50-k that relate specifically to the City of New York? 24
   What laws cover the indemnification of Corrections employees? 25
   Are PUNITIVE DAMAGES covered by the indemnification laws? 26
   Can law enforcement officers sue third parties for injuries suffered in the performance of duty? 27

What is the "firefighter's rule" and does it apply to New
  York law enforcement officers? 27
Firefighter's Rule Modified to Permit Some Law Suits 30
New Constitutional Tort Created In New York 32

Part III - FEDERAL CIVIL RIGHTS ACTIONS 35
What is a "Section 1983" action? 35
What are the elements of a "Section 1983" action? 35
When is an officer "acting under color of law?" 36
What are some of the constitutional rights that are
  commonly used as the basis of a "Section 1983" action?
  36
Can supervisors be held liable for the actions of a
  subordinate? 37
Can a municipality be held liable under Section 1983? 39
How can an agency be held liable for "failure to train"? ... 40
What are the defenses of "absolute immunity" and
  "qualified immunity?" 41
Can "Ride-along" situations violate the Fourth Amendment?
  43
Can an officer be prosecuted for criminal acts for violating
  a person's civil rights? 44

Endnotes 47

Index 51

Introduction

As always, the issue of civil liability remains a serious problem for law enforcement officers. In this newly updated and revised First Edition of the Guide, materials have been expanded relating to liability for failure to protect an individual ("special relationship" cases), the "firefighter rule," supervisor liability under federal constitutional law and qualified immunity. In addition, a new section was added dealing with agency liability for failure to train.

Police officers, sheriffs, correction officers and other peace officers are called upon each day to exercise discretion and are vulnerable to being sued in a wide variety of situations. Lawsuits may arise under claims of negligence, unlawful use of force, false arrest, invasions of privacy, search and seizure, deprivation of constitutional rights and many other theories. However, just because a lawsuit is filed does not mean that the officer acted wrongfully; the issue of liability is one to be resolved by a judge or jury.

Civil lawsuits generally seek money damages, although sometimes other forms of relief may be sought. If money damages are awarded, there is concern by officers as to whether or not they alone are responsible to pay or is there some form of indemnification. Fortunately, as noted below, there is indemnification in most cases. Supervisors and governmental agencies may also be liable for the acts of the officers or for their own failure to perform properly.

Some wrongful acts by an officer, such as assault, may involve criminal liability as well as civil liability. There is also a potential for criminal liability under federal laws for certain deprivation of constitutional rights.

The materials presented in this outline are based on questions raised over the years during training sessions conducted by the authors with law enforcement recruits and supervisors. The responses reflect the best judgment of the author and are not intended as legal advice in specific cases.

John J. Sullivan   January, 2000
Lt. Michael D. Ranalli   November 2005

About the Authors

John Sullivan retired in 1999 from his position as a Professor of Law and Criminal Justice at Mercy College, Dobbs Ferry, New York., where he also served as Chairman of the Department of Law, Criminal Justice and Safety Administration. After twenty-two years of service, he retired from the New York City Police Department as Captain and Director of the Legal Division. He also served as Professor and Associate Dean of Professional Studies at John Jay College of Criminal Justice, CUNY. He authored several publications relating to criminal justice and law enforcement, including "The Laws of Search and Seizure For New York Law Enforcement Officers." He was active in public affairs and served as Chair of the Westchester County Criminal Justice Advisory Board and also served on the Board of Directors of the Legal Aid Society of Westchester County. John Sullivan died in 2001 and is missed by many.

Michael Ranalli is a Lieutenant with the Colonie, New York Police Department. He has been a police officer for 21 years and is also an attorney, having graduated from Albany Law School in 1991. He has been involved in police training for the last 15 years and lectures on topics including civil liability, search and seizure, stop and frisk, 5th and 6th amendments, use of force and a variety of other areas of criminal procedure.

Part I
DEFINITIONS

What is a TORT?

A TORT is a private or civil wrong or injury, other than a breach of contract, for which a court will provide a remedy in the form of an action for damages.

A TORT is distinguishable from a criminal proceeding which involves a public wrong and is prosecuted in the name of "The People."

There are three elements which must be established for every TORT action:

 i) Existence of a legal duty between defendant and plaintiff,
 ii) Breach of duty, and
 iii) damages as a proximate result.

A **CONSTITUTIONAL TORT** involves a violation of rights protected by the U.S. Constitution or Federal law. (See Section 1983 Actions, page 35 and the discussion concerning State Constitutional Torts, page 33).

An **INTENTIONAL TORT**, as contrasted with **NEGLIGENCE**, is one in which the actor intends to do that which the law has declared wrong.

What is NEGLIGENCE?

NEGLIGENCE is the breach of a duty to act reasonably towards others. It could be the **omission** to do something which a reasonable person, guided by those ordinary considerations which regulate human affairs, would do or **the doing of something** which a reasonable or prudent person would not do.

What are DAMAGES?

COMPENSATORY DAMAGES are such damages as will compensate a party for the injury sustained, and nothing more. They are awarded as compensation, indemnity or restitution for harm and may include out-of-pocket expenses, loss of earning power and pain and suffering.

PUNITIVE DAMAGES are damages awarded over and above COMPENSATORY DAMAGES. They are awarded as **punishment** when the wrong done was aggravated by circumstances of violence, fraud, malice, oppression or wanton or wicked conduct.

NOMINAL DAMAGES are a trifling sum awarded when there has been no substantial loss or damages but the law recognizes a violation of rights. Sometimes referred to as a $.06 award.

What does INDEMNIFICATION mean?

INDEMNIFICATION occurs when another party, such as an employer or insurance company, pays the damages awarded against an individual.

What does RESPONDEAT SUPERIOR mean?

RESPONDEAT SUPERIOR means "let the master answer." Under this doctrine, the employer is responsible for the wrongful acts of its employees. Generally, this doctrine does not apply if the employee was acting outside the legitimate scope of authority.

Part II
CIVIL LIABILITY UNDER NEW YORK LAW

This section will provide an overview of those areas of civil liability of most concern to New York law enforcement officers. A review of the special laws of New York which provide for indemnification for certain torts will be presented.

What are some of the consequences to an officer for wrongful conduct?

An officer who engages in wrongful conduct faces the possibility of internal departmental discipline, a state lawsuit, state criminal charges, federal civil law suit and federal criminal charges. The fact that an officer is absolved from criminal charges does not bar the agency from bringing disciplinary charges for the same action and, as was seen in the Rodney King case in California, an acquittal on state criminal charges does not bar federal criminal charges for the same actions. In addition to the various levels of procedural and legal scrutiny discussed above there is also a more intangible aspect. Internal investigations and law suits can be a tremendous source of stress on the family as well as the officer. While any officer can be sued at any time, even when it may seem unjustified, there is one general rule that can help officers get through their careers unscathed – never act with **malice**.

What are some of the liability issues concerning the operation of MOTOR VEHICLES?

Officers are held to the same standard of care as ordinary citizens when operating their vehicles. When on emergency runs, certain traffic regulations may be ignored, but care is still required. In 1995, the Court of Appeals indicated that the standard of care to be applied to the operation of emergency vehicles is the **reckless disregard standard**. "This standard demands more than a showing of a lack of 'due care under the circumstances...'" It requires evidence that the 'actor has intentionally done an act of an unreasonable character in disregard of an known or obvious risk that was so great as to make it highly probable that harm would follow' and has done so with conscious disregard to the outcome."[1]

Causing an accident by excessive speed or entering intersections without looking may be the basis for a negligence action, notwithstanding the use of siren and lights.[2]

The operator of a pursuing emergency vehicle may be found liable for injuries to a third party caused by the pursued vehicle if the court finds that the emergency vehicle was operated in "reckless disregard for the safety of others." In *Thain v. City of New York*,[3] the court held that failure of police officers to sound their sirens or operate their flashing lights during pursuit of a traffic violator was a proximate cause of a intersection collision between the fleeing vehicle and the vehicle of the injured plaintiff.

In May, 1998, the U.S. Supreme Court reviewed a claim brought under 42 U.S.C. §1983 for wrongful death arising out of a situation where a pursuing police vehicle struck and killed a young man.[4] The man had been a passenger on a motorcycle which was being pursued. The motorcycle skidded, the victim fell off, and the police vehicle could not avoid hitting him.

One of the issues was what standard of liability applied in such cases. The Court discussed such standards as mere negligence, gross negligence and deliberate and reckless indifference.

However, this case involved more than a claim based on negligence, but rather, it was a claim for a violation of civil rights . As the Court stated "The issue in this case is whether a police officer violates the *Fourteenth Amendment's* guarantee of substantive due process by causing death through deliberate or reckless indifference to life in a high speed automobile chase aimed at apprehending a suspected offender. **We answer no, and hold that in such circumstances only a purpose to cause harm unrelated to the legitimate object of arrest will satisfy the element of arbitrary conduct shocking to the conscience, necessary for a due process violation."** (emphasis added).

This decision does not impact on the standard set for New York in negligence as indicated above. This "shocks the conscience" standard is significantly higher than the "reckless disregard" New York standard. Therefore, depending upon how serious the facts of a particular case, officers are more likely to be sued in New York courts for motor vehicle accidents.

Indemnification: General Municipal Law §50-c provides that the employing municipality shall assume the liability of and save harmless its police officers for the negligent operation of a motor vehicle in the line of duty. (GML §50-k covers the City of New York.)

What consideration should be given to the establishment of a roadblock?

Special care must be exercised in the setting up of a roadblock. The Supreme Court has held that the establishment of a roadblock is a "seizure" within the meaning of the Fourth Amendment.[5] A roadblock should be employed as a last resort and then only in serious cases. It is suggested that a supervisor be required to authorize its establishment and pursuing officers must be made aware of its location.

A roadblock should afford approaching vehicles an opportunity to stop and an avenue of escape from collision. The negligent establishment of a roadblock which causes injury to the suspect or an innocent party may be the basis of liability. Department guidelines should be established and followed. The use of a road block can be considered an application of deadly physical force.

What standards govern the USE OF FORCE by the police?

It is generally accepted that the police may use reasonable force when necessary to maintain the peace or to make an arrest or legal stop. What constitutes reasonable force for the purpose of a civil suit depends on the circumstances of each case. Some of the factors that will be considered are:

a. The seriousness of the crime;
b. Whether the suspect is actively resisting arrest or attempting to evade arrest by flight;
c. Whether the suspect poses an immediate threat to the safety of the officer or others.

In *Graham v. Connor*,[6] the Supreme Court stated that "...the appropriateness of the force used to accomplish [a] seizure must be assessed in the context of the 'reasonableness' standard." The officer's state of mind is not a factor in establishing reasonableness but the question is rather "whether the officer's actions are 'objectively reasonable' in light of the facts and circumstances confronting them, without regard to their underlying intent or motivation." While *Graham* pertains to federal claims, the standards set forth are similar to those required under New York law.

Every case presents its own fact pattern. The burden of proving that excessive force was used lies with the plaintiff. Once that happens, the burden shifts to the defendant (officer) to show that the use of force was reasonable and justified.

Does Article 35 of the Penal Law set the standards in a civil case concerning the use of force?

No. Article 35 of the New York Penal Law establishes the defense of "Justification" in a criminal proceeding and sets forth the circumstances under which the use of physical force by anyone would be justified and not criminal. §35.30 relates to the authorized use of physical force, including deadly physical force, by police and/or peace officers in making an arrest or preventing escape.

In April 1993, the New York Court of Appeals sustained a $4.3 million verdict awarded a plaintiff who was permanently paralyzed from the mid-chest down when he was shot by a New York City Transit Police Officer.[7] The plaintiff was unarmed and running away from the scene of an attempted robbery in which he was a participant when he was shot by the officer. The theory of the plaintiff's case, as was submitted to the jury, was common law negligence, i.e., that the officer by employing deadly physical force in an attempt to apprehend the plaintiff did not exercise that degree of care which would be reasonably required of a police officer under similar circumstances. The majority of the Court of Appeals found that there was a factual basis for the jury verdict, holding that the most favorable view of the evidence for the plaintiff established that the officer did not see the mugging and did not know whether a violent crime had been threatened or committed.

The Court rejected the argument that the shooting was justified under Penal Law §35.30, holding that this section of law relates to justification under the criminal law and was not applicable in this case. It likewise refused to hold that the U.S. Supreme Court decision in *Tennessee v. Garner*,[8] justified the officer's actions. *Garner* "establishes the minimum standard of care which a police officer must exercise in making an arrest to avoid violation of the arrestee's Fourth Amendment rights." It did not establish a shield of immunity for the defendant in a common law negligence action.

Two dissenting judges would have found the action reasonable under Penal Law §35.30 and the *Garner* and *Graham* cases.

What is the case of *Tennessee v. Garner*, referred to in the previous question?

In the case of *Tennessee v. Garner* the Supreme Court placed a Constitutional limitation on the use of deadly physical force. The case involved a fatal police shooting of a fleeing, unarmed, burglar. The Court said, "... We conclude that such force may not be used unless it is necessary to prevent the escape and the officer has probable cause to believe that the suspected person poses a significant threat of death or serious physical injury to the officer or others..." and that "...there can be no question that the apprehension by the use of deadly physical force is a seizure subject to the reasonableness requirements of the Fourth Amendment..."

The Court also stated that:

"...Where the police officer has probable cause to believe that the suspect poses a threat of serious physical harm, either to the officer or to others, it is not constitutionally unreasonable to prevent escape by using deadly force. Thus, if the suspect threatens the officer with a weapon or there is probable cause to believe that he has committed a crime involving the infliction or threatened infliction of serious physical harm, deadly physical force may be used if necessary to prevent escape, and if feasible, some warning has been given."

NOTE: The use of warnings shots is not recommended. Department procedures should be followed.

Garner establishes the minimum standard of care to avoid a violation of the suspect's Fourth Amendment rights. What is not clear, is the impact of this decision on Penal Law §35.30. This section has not been amended to reflect the limitations of *Garner*. For example, Penal Law §35.30(1)(a)(i) states that deadly physical force may be used when an officer reasonably believes that a felony or an attempt to commit a felony involving the use or attempted use or threatened imminent use of physical force against a person. This language would arguably justify the use of deadly force against a person who just committed a purse snatching. This clearly would violate the limitations of *Garner*. Fortunately, most police agencies have amended their procedures to limit the use of deadly physical force to those situations involving self defense and danger to others when there is the possibility of serious physical injury or death being inflicted.

What are some of the INTENTIONAL TORTS that involve police action?

a) **Assault and Battery**

Any willful attempt or threat to inflict injury upon the person of another, when coupled with the apparent present ability to do so, and any intentional display of force such as would give the victim reason to fear or expect immediate bodily harm, constitutes ASSAULT. (cf.. Menacing, Penal Law, Art. 120.)

BATTERY constitutes the infliction of harmful body contact. (Cf.. Assault, Penal Law, Art.120.)

Civil suits against officers for assault and battery take on many forms ranging from wrongful death to simple handling and handcuffing of a person. In some cases the damages awarded can be substantial.

In March 1986, two men were driving on the streets of Coney Island in New York City at 11:40 PM when their car was blockaded by undercover police officers in unmarked cars. The police fired shots into the air, dragged the men out of the car and beat them. The police said they thought the men were robbery suspects and when the driver, Mr. Papa, tried to maneuver his car, he struck a police vehicle. The men were charged with attempted murder and denied food and medical attention for several hours. Mr. Papa was a local attorney and civic leader and all charges against him and his companion were dismissed on the District Attorney's motion.

The men sued the officers and the City of New York for assault and battery, negligence, false arrest, malicious prosecution and civil rights violations. A jury awarded $76 million in compensatory and punitive damages. The trial judge reduced the award to $6.1 million and in June 1993, the Appellate Division, Second

Department, further reduced the award to $5.6 million which included $500,000 in punitive damages for each plaintiff.[9]

b) False Arrest/False Imprisonment

False imprisonment is an unlawful detention contrary to the will of the person detained, accomplished with or without process of law. False arrest is a detention accomplished by means of an unlawful arrest, and is a trespass against the person arrested.

The elements of an action in false arrest are:

(i) the defendant intended to confine the plaintiff
(ii) the plaintiff was conscious of the confinement,
(iii) the plaintiff did not consent to the confinement, and
(iv) the confinement was not otherwise privileged.

It is important that officers fully understand the law of arrest as set forth in the Criminal Procedure Law. While the law protects the officer who acts with "reasonable cause to believe," an officer must be aware of the legal limitations in the statutes and in court decisions.

In July, 1993, the Appellate Division, First Department, ruled that a plaintiff was entitled to summary judgment in her action for false arrest. The plaintiff was a passenger in a car lawfully traveling across 42nd Street in Manhattan early in the morning. The car was stopped by undercover police, allegedly because of a loose rear license plate, and both she and the driver got out. An officer reached into the car's interior and recovered a black bag from which he retrieved a .22 caliber revolver. Both were arrested despite the driver's claim that the plaintiff was innocent. She was detained for two days and released on her own recognizance. The Prosecution moved to dismiss the complaint **conceding the search and seizure of the gun was illegal.**

The appellate panel found there "was no triable issue of fact remaining for the jury to decide." The City of New York argued that the confinement was privileged because there was probable cause for the arrest even if the search was unlawful. The Court disagreed, stating:

> "We disagree. The fruit of an illegal search cannot give rise, in a juristic sense, to probable cause to arrest and the conceded illegality of the search and seizure is thus conclusive against the defendant on the issue of privilege... Were this not so, the police could subject a person to an egregiously unconstitutional search and then use that search to establish, in a civil suit for false imprisonment, that the arrest was based on probable cause. The absurdity of such a principle is so patent as to require no further discussion."[10]

Malicious Prosecution

The essence of a **malicious prosecution** action is that it is begun in malice, without probable cause to believe it can succeed.

The elements of an action for malicious prosecution are:

(i)   The commencement or continuance of a proceeding by the defendant against the plaintiff,
(ii) the termination of that proceeding in favor of the plaintiff,
(iii) the absence of probable cause for the proceeding, and
(iv) actual malice.

Police officers are subject to liability for malicious prosecution when they knowingly initiate a prosecution on less than probable cause. Liability has been found where, after an arrest based on probable cause took place, the officer filed a perjured felony complaint alleging that the defendant was identified in a lineup by victims. Such a line-up never took place and the defendant was able to establish his innocence.[11]

In 1991, Manuel Morillo was arrested in Manhattan and charged with criminal possession of a controlled substance and criminal possession of a weapon. Morillo was convicted and sentenced to prison. Three years later it was discovered that the two arresting officers committed perjury and one admitted that he never saw defendant with drugs and did not find a weapon in his possession. Morillo and his wife brought suit in federal court for malicious prosecution, false imprisonment and for violation of 42 U.S.C. §1983. In February, 1997, District Judge Martin held that Morillo had established the requisite elements of the tort of false imprisonment and malicious prosecution and for violation of §1983. The only issue remaining for trial was the establishment of damages.[12]

Are law enforcement officers or their agencies liable for failure to protect an individual?

Generally, there is no liability for failure to protect an individual. The police owe a duty to the public but not to each individual. However, liability to an individual may arise if a **"special relationship"** exists.

The Court of Appeals, in *Cuffy v. City of New York*,[13] stated that the essential elements necessary to establish the "special relationship" are:

(i) "an assumption by the municipality, through promises or actions, of an affirmative duty to act on behalf of the party who was injured;

(ii)   knowledge on the part of the municipality's agents that inaction could lead to harm;
(iii) some form of direct contact between the municipality's agents and the injured party;
(iv)   the party's justifiable reliance on the municipality's affirmative undertaking."

In *Sorichetti v. City of New York*,[14] the City was held liable for the injuries suffered by an infant at the hands of her father. The father was an abusive spouse and Mrs. Sorichetti obtained a final Order of Protection which required the father to stay away from the house. However, the Court ordered that the father could have visitation rights with his six year old daughter from 10:00 AM Saturday to 6:00 PM Sunday and the child was to be picked up and delivered at the precinct station house. On the first visit, as the father was leaving with the child, he uttered a threat to Mrs. Sorichetti and the child. The mother reported this to the desk officer and asked that her husband be arrested for violating the Order of Protection. The desk officer refused. On the next day, Mrs. Sorichetti again asked that the husband be arrested and that the child be returned. Even after being advised by another officer that Mr. Sorichetti was very violent, the desk officer refused to take any action. On that day, the child was violently attacked by her father and suffered permanent physical damages. The father was convicted of attempted murder.

The jury found that the police department breached a special duty of care owed to the child when it refused to act on the mother's complaints. A "special relationship" arose out of the Order of Protection, the knowledge of Mr. Sorichetti's violent temper, Mrs. Sorichetti's reasonable expectation of protection and the police response to the mother's request for help. A $2 million award was affirmed.

Although the *Sorichetti* case made it clear that the "fact that an injury occurs because of a violation of an order of protection does not in itself create municipal liability," it did indicate that there may be circumstances under which such relationship may be created. In another "Order of Protection" case, *Mastroianni v. County of Suffolk*,[15] the court found that a "special relationship" was established.

Mrs. Mastroianni had a permanent order of protection against her husband. The husband was arrested on June 24, 1985, for violating the order of protection, less than two weeks after it was issued. On the evening of September 5, 1985, the Suffolk County Police responded to a 911 call from Mrs. Mastroianni that her husband had violated the order by entering her home and throwing furniture out on the lawn. When the officers arrived there was furniture on the front lawn but the husband was not there. He was at a next door neighbor's home. He denied entering his wife's home and removing furniture. No witnesses came forward putting him at the scene. There were no outstanding warrants and a supervising officer advised the officers that since the husband was not seen at the scene they should not arrest him. Mrs. Mastroianni was upset and pleaded with the officers to arrest her husband saying she was "afraid of this man." As the officers let the husband go, one of them said to him ...."if I had to come back here again tonight, if there are any further problems, that he would be arrested and taken to jail." The officers remained at the scene for about an hour when they left on a meal break. A few minutes after they left, the husband returned and stabbed his wife to death.

In an action to recover damages for decedent's death, Defendants moved for Summary Judgement and the Supreme Court denied the motion. The Appellate Division reversed and dismissed the complaint holding that there was no special duty owed to the decedent and that the officers actions were reasonable.

The Court of Appeals reversed the Appellate Division finding that "the elements of a special relationship as set forth in *Cuffy* were present here. The existence of an order of protection, the extended contact of the police with the decedent and the decedent's justifiable reliance on the officers' affirmative undertaking on her behalf all serve to demonstrate that a special relationship was established here." The Court further held that there was a question of fact concerning the reasonableness of the officers' actions and the case was remanded back to the trial court for an examination of the evidence.

Mastroianni relaxes the *Cuffy* requirement as to justifiable reliance on police protection by allowing the expectation of the party seeking protection, and not the physical location of the police, as the deciding factor in creating justifiable reliance.

A contrary result was reached in *Kircher v. City of Jamestown*.[16] The plaintiff, Deborah Kircher, was accosted and kidnapped by a man from a store parking lot. Two people witnessed the incident, gave chase but lost sight of the vehicle. They came across a Jamestown police officer and told him of the events, the suspect vehicle license plate number and description. The officer said he would call it in but he never did. The victim was beaten and raped and locked in the trunk of her car for 12 hours.

She sued the officer and the City of Jamestown for negligence in failing to render assistance. The City moved to dismiss the complaint because there was no "special relationship" between herself and the City and the trial court refused. The Appellate Division reversed and the Court of Appeals affirmed the reversal.

The Court found that in this case "neither the requirement of direct contact nor of justifiable reliance has been satisfied."

The existence of an order of protection significantly reduces the burden of proof for a plaintiff to show a special relationship was established. "In short, the order satisfies proof of an affirmative duty to act, knowledge that inaction could lead to harm and justifiable reliance on the defendant's affirmative undertaking. All that remains is the direct contact necessary to apprise the police of the existence of the order and its violation."[17] This places a severe burden on officers investigating incidents involving orders of protection. Officers should be aggressive in such investigations and make arrests when appropriate.

In March of 2005 the U.S. Supreme Court decided the case of *Town of Castle Rock, Colorado v. Gonzales*.[18] A brief discussion of this case is warranted more for what it does **not** stand for as compared to what it does. It is important officers understand the distinction as the holding of the case could be misinterpreted. Mrs. Gonzales had a permanent restraining order against her husband. On June 22, 1999 the husband took the children while they were playing outside their home. This was in violation of the order and Mrs. Gonzales contacted the police several times during the night requesting assistance. The police made no attempt to investigate or enforce the order. At about 3:20 a.m. the husband went to the police station and opened fire with a semiautomatic handgun he had just purchased. He was shot and killed by officers who then found all three of the Gonzales children murdered in the husband's truck. The wife brought a civil rights action under 42 U.S.C. §1983 claiming, among other things, that under the Due Process Clause of the 14th Amendment she had a property interest in the police enforcement of the restraining order against her husband. The Supreme Court disagreed and effectively dismissed her case. At first glance this would appear to contradict the case law discussed previously. The cases previously discussed in this section were **tort** actions in which the plaintiffs attempted to prove a breach of a duty. The *Castle Rock* case only stands for the proposition that the Due Process clause does not mandate enforcement of restraining orders and is therefore not the appropriate legal remedy in such cases. This case does not in any way prohibit law suits for negligence as in *Sorichetti* and *Cuffy* and does not relax the burden on officers when investigating such calls.

911 Calls: While at first blush it would seem that a 911 call would meet the "special relationship" test, New York has held that a call made by a third party that there was a disturbance and screams coming from an apartment did not establish the "direct contact" requirement to allow the occupant of the apartment to sue because of negligent police response.[19] However, if a person calls 911 directly and is injured because of negligent police response, liability may arise.[20]

Liability may also arise "even when no original duty is owed to the plaintiff to undertake affirmative action, once it is voluntarily undertaken it must be performed with due care."[21]

In a 1997 decision, the Appellate Division, Fourth Department held that a "special relationship" was created when police stopped a vehicle and arrested the driver for driving while intoxicated. Jacqueline Walsh, owner of the vehicle, was a passenger in the vehicle and the police determined that she also was intoxicated and unable to drive safely. An Alcosensor test indicated that her blood alcohol concentration was .16%. The police offered to call a cab or drive her to any destination she wanted. She refused and she left the scene on foot. About fifteen minutes later, Walsh was killed by a train as she was crossing railroad tracks about 35 feet from where her car was stopped. Her representatives brought a wrongful death action alleging that the officers were negligent in removing her from her vehicle and leaving her stranded, in a visibly intoxicated condition, on a dark road within 35 feet of a railroad track at 5:30 in the morning. The Town argued that there was no "special relationship" with Walsh. The Court, one Judge dissenting, disagreed and held that the question of negligence was one for a trial jury to determine.[22]

In *Thomas v. City of Auburn*,[23] the Court found there was a special relationship created with patrons of a bar who were assaulted (one fatally) by an unruly patron, Jimmy Rouse. Rouse had been ejected from the bar and threatened to return and kill the others. The police were called and the officers who responded promised to remain and escort the patrons from the premises when they finished repairing the window broken by Rouse. However, without advising the others they were leaving, the officers left to look for Rouse. While they were gone, Rouse returned and shot the victims.

Are officers liable to injured third parties for failure to arrest intoxicated drivers?

The general rule in New York is that officers are not liable to third persons for failure to arrest intoxicated drivers who subsequently get involved in accidents with the third person.

The courts rely on the "public duty" and "special relationship" rules referred to above.[24]

What are the laws relating to indemnification?

State Employees

§17 of the Public Officers Law provides for the defense and indemnification for employees of New York State. The section provides for the furnishing of counsel and subdivision 3(a) states:

> The state shall indemnify and save harmless its employees in the amount of any judgment obtained against such employees in any state or federal court, or in the amount of any settlement of a claim, or shall pay such judgment or settlement; provided that the act or omission from which such judgment or settlement arose occurred while the employee was acting within the scope of his public employment or duties; the duty to indemnify and save harmless or pay prescribed by this subdivision shall not arise where the injury or damage resulted from intentional wrongdoing on the part of the employee.

As the result of an 1986 amendment, the prohibition against the payment of punitive or exemplary damages was deleted from this section.

Municipal Employees

The principal laws relating to the indemnification of employees of counties, cities, towns, villages, etc. are contained in Public Officers Law §18 and Article 4 of the General Municipal Law. POL §18 is a comprehensive indemnification law that relates to employees of public entities other than the State of New York. It authorizes the public entity to provide indemnification and a defense for any incident "arising out of any alleged act or omission which occurred or allegedly occurred while the employee was acting within the scope of his public employment or duties." It specifically prohibits the payment of punitive damages. Officers should be aware of any local laws that relate to indemnification, such as Westchester County Administrative Code, §297.31, subdivision 4(b), which provides that the duty to indemnify shall not arise when the injury or damages resulted from intentional wrongdoing or recklessness on the part of the employee.

In *Polak v. City of Schenectady*,[25] the court reviewed the action of the city's Corporation Counsel refusing to furnish a defense to an officer being sued by another officer on the grounds that the first officer was not acting within the scope of his employment. The civil suit for assault and mental distress alleged the two officers were on duty in the vice-squad office of the police department when officer Polak twice placed a loaded gun to the forehead of the other officer. The Corporation Counsel, pursuant to POL §18, reviewed the facts and determined that the actions were not in the scope of the employee's duties and refused indemnification and defense. The Appellate Division affirmed.

GML §§50-a, 50-b, 50-c concern municipal liability for the negligent operation of motor vehicles. GML §50-e is an important section. It requires that the claimant file a Notice of Claim with the municipality within 90 days after the claim arises, except in wrongful death, where the service must be within 90 days of the appointment of a representative of the estate. §50-I requires the commencement of the action within one year and 90 days after the event (two years in wrongful death cases). Failure to comply with these sections can result in a lawsuit being barred.

There are two sections 50-j in the General Municipal Law. The first relates to police officers and the other to correction officers employed by cities. The section relating to police provides that the employer shall be liable, and shall assume the liability to the extent that it shall save harmless any duly appointed police officer of such municipality, etc., for any negligent act or tort, provided such police officer, at the time of the negligent act or tort complained of, was acting in the performance of his duties and within the scope of his employment. **Note**: this section does not apply to the City of New York; see discussion which follows referring to GML §50-k.

Is an officer indemnified if he/she takes police action while OFF-DUTY?

GML §50-j (2) refers to **off-duty** situations. It provides that a police officer, "although excused from official duty at the time, shall be deemed to be acting in the discharge of duty when engaged in the immediate and actual performance of a public duty imposed by law and such public duty was for the benefit of the citizens of the community wherein the such public duty was performed..."

In order for an off-duty officer to be protected by the indemnification provisions, the officer will have to establish that he/she was performing a public duty, such as trying to prevent a crime or to make a lawful arrest or carrying out some other required duty. In the case of *Wilson v. City of N.Y.*,[26] an off-duty officer was driving a taxicab when he saw a crime in progress and he jumped from the cab to take preventative action. However, the cab continued to roll and the passenger within was injured. The passenger sued the officer and the City for negligence and the court determined that the officer was acting in the performance of a public duty when he left the cab. However, the passenger failed to file her negligence claim within the one year and 90 days as required by GML §50-I and §50-j(3) and the court barred her suit against both the City and the off-duty officer. In *Desa v. City of N.Y.*,[27] the court held that the City could be held liable for injuries caused by an off-duty officer negligently cleaning his revolver, holding that such action was within the scope of the officer's employment.

In *Joseph v. City of Buffalo*,[28] the City was not liable for injuries suffered by a police officer's child, when the child shot himself at home with the officer's service revolver. Although the officer was negligent and failed to comply with instructions concerning the safeguarding of his gun, he was not engaged in any police business while at home with his family and the city could not be held vicariously liable for his conduct.

An officer will not be protected if the court finds he/she was engaged in a private enterprise. In *Stavitz v. City of N.Y.*,[29] action was brought against the City for assault, false arrest and malicious prosecution arising out of a police officer's assault of a neighbor and his son. The relations between the officer and his neighbor had been unpleasant, marked by arguments and cursing. On the day in issue, the off-duty officer entered his neighbor's home, they argued and the officer assaulted both the neighbor and his son and then departed. Several minutes later, he returned to the home and displaying his shield, he placed the neighbor and his son under arrest, charging assault and resisting arrest. The two were acquitted after a non-jury trial.

In their civil action, the jury found that the officer was acting within the scope of his employment and in furtherance of the City's business and awarded damages. On appeal, the Appellate Division reversed as to the City's liability. The court found that the officer was acting for purely private reasons, even when he effected the arrest.[30]

What are the provisions of GML 50-k that relate specifically to the City of New York?

The present version of GML §50-k was enacted in 1979. Basically, the statute provides that New York City employees who properly perform their duties and are subsequently sued shall be entitled to representation by the Corporation Counsel and any resulting judgment or settlement shall be paid by the City. The statute specifically includes actions in federal court under Section 1983 of Title 42, U.S.C. The employee shall not be entitled to the statute's indemnification protection if the actions complained of were in violation of any rule or regulation of the agency or where the injury or damages resulted from intentional wrongdoing or recklessness on part of the employee. This would seem to preclude indemnification for punitive damages.

The statute also requires the employee to cooperate with the Corporation Counsel by delivering all papers served on the employee promptly and otherwise assisting in the defense of the action. Failure to cooperate can be cause for the Corporation Counsel to withdraw representation. The law further provides that if the actions of the employee are also the basis of disciplinary charges representation by the Corporation Counsel and indemnification may be withheld until the disciplinary proceedings are resolved and the resolution exonerates the employee. If the employee is not exonerated, the City will refuse to furnish a defense or indemnification.

This statute was applied in the case of former Police Officer Francis X. Livoti. In December, 1994, Livoti, while on duty, in uniform, was involved in an altercation with Anthony Baez. Mr. Baez died after the officer applied an illegal choke hold. Officer Livoti was acquitted of criminally negligent homicide in state court in 1996 but was convicted in Federal Court in June 1998 for violating Mr. Baez's civil rights. In October, 1998, he was sentenced to 7½ years in prison.. After the state trial, Livoti was fired from the Police Department for violating Departmental regulations.

Baez's family brought a civil action against Livoti, the Police Department and the City of New York. The City was permitted to deny a defense to Livoti because he was facing disciplinary charges arising from the death of Mr. Baez at the time the action was filed. The City also tried to argue that it did not have to indemnify Livoti because he was acting outside of the scope of his employment. The court rejected this argument, finding that "the events that gave rise to the tragic death of Anthony Baez was part and parcel of a police enterprise." The City has settled the law suit for three million dollars.[31]

What laws cover the indemnification of Corrections employees?

Corrections Law §24 provides that no lawsuit can be brought in state court against an officer or employee of the Department of Correctional Services, in his/her personal capacity, for damages arising out of the performance of duty. Such an action must be brought against the State in the Court of Claims.

GML 50-j (set out second) provides similar protection for corrections employees of cities.

These statutes provide immunity from being sued rather than indemnification.[32]

Are **PUNITIVE DAMAGES** covered by the indemnification laws?

Yes and No.

The New York Court of Appeals has stated that it would be against the public policy of the State to allow insurance companies to pay punitive damages awarded against an insured.[33] The Court argued that to allow indemnification would defeat the "purposes of punitive damages, which is to punish and deter others from acting similarly..." However, following a suggestion made by the Court of Appeals,[34] the New York Legislature has adopted several laws that establish a "public policy" which permits the payment of punitive damages in certain cases.

As noted above, POL §17 was amended to allow the payment of punitive damages in cases involving State employees. GML §50-j was amended in 1986 by adding a new subdivision 6 which permits municipalities to adopt local laws or resolutions to allow the indemnification of police officers for awards of punitive damages. It also permits the purchase of insurance to cover such claims. Few, if any, municipalities have adopted such laws so that most local officers are not covered for punitive damages. However, special laws have been adopted that cover law enforcement officers in Nassau and Suffolk counties. GML §50-l provides for the defense and indemnification of police officers of the Nassau County Police Department, including **punitive damages**. The statute calls for the creation of a special panel to determine if the officer was acting in the proper discharge of duties. GML §50-n provides similar protection to a duly appointed peace officer, sheriff, undersheriff or deputy sheriff of Nassau County. GML §50-m provides similar protection to a duly appointed police officer or peace officer of Suffolk County.

Can law enforcement officers sue third parties for injuries suffered in the performance of duty?

An officer can sue for intentional torts, such as assault and malicious prosecution, for negligence, and for defamation (libel and/or slander).

Defamation cases are difficult to establish. Law enforcement officers are "public officials" and, under the rule of *Sullivan v. New York Times*,[35] in order to recover damages it must be proven that the false statement was made with **malice**, that is, uttered with knowledge that it was false or made with a reckless disregard of the truth or falsity of the statement.

The right to sue a third person for negligence might be curtailed by the **"firefighter's rule."**

What is the "firefighter's rule" and does it apply to New York law enforcement officers?

The **"firefighter's rule"** is a common-law rule that holds that firefighters injured in the line of duty can not recover from the owners or occupants of property whose negligence caused the fire emergency to which they were responding. To offset the harshness of this rule, the Legislature, in 1935, enacted General Municipal Law §205-a which gave firefighters a statutory cause of action for line-of-duty injuries arising out of culpable negligence in a party's failure to comply with statutes, rules, ordinances, etc.

In 1988, the Court of Appeals applied the common-law "firefighter's rule"[36] to police officers, since they, like firefighters, "are experts engaged, trained and compensated by the public to deal on its behalf with emergencies and hazards often created by negligence." The Legislature responded by enacting General Municipal Law §205-e to afford police officers with the same right to sue as firefighters in case of negligent failure to comply with statutes, ordinances, rules, etc.

In 1999 the Court of Appeals refused to extend the firefighter's rule to New York City sanitation workers.[37]

In the ensuing years there have been a number of court decisions that have tried to apply these statutes and to avoid the harshness of the "firefighter's rule." However, the rule was still a barrier to many causes of action.[38]

In order to make a claim under §205-e a potential plaintiff must accomplish three things. First the statute or ordinance that the defendant failed to comply with must be identified. Second, the manner in which the officer was injured must be described. Finally, the plaintiff must show from the facts that the defendant's negligence directly or indirectly caused his or her harm.[39] If any of these three requirements could not be met then the "firefighter's rule" would prohibit the action.

At first blush these requirements would seem fairly easy to meet. The statute or ordinance in question, however, must be one that is a "well developed body of law and regulation that imposes clear duties."[40] Over the last few years a number of cases have held that the alleged statutory violation was insufficient to meet this burden. For example, violation of a City Patrol Guide was held to be insufficient since it is intended to be more of a guide for officers rather than a prescription of specific actions that must be taken when faced with specific situations.[41] In *Williams v. City of New York* and it's companion case of *McCormick v. City of New York*,[42] the plaintiffs also failed to prove the required statutory violation. *McCormick* involved a sergeant who was killed by a bullet fired by another officer struggling with an armed subject in another room. The plaintiff argued that §35.30 of the Penal Law, dealing with the defense of justification, was violated by the officer who fired the fatal shot. This did not meet the requirement of §205-e that requires a law that sets forth "clear duties." The defense of justification set forth in §35.30 is fact driven on a case by case basis and requires the scrutiny of the decisions of officers made in fractions of a second and therefore does not establish "clear duties." The court held that no other penal law violations appear to have occurred since the defendants in the case were not charged with any such violations.

Williams involved two officers who were shot and killed by a subject in a station house interview room. The room doubled as a locker room and the subject was able to obtain a gun from a locker. The plaintiffs, the officers survivors, claimed, among other things, that the City violated the "general duty" clause of Labor Law §27-a (the Public Employee Safety and Health Act) that requires that employers provide a hazard free workplace. The Court of Appeals held that this law does not cover the special risks inherent in police work. Police supervisors, rather than Department of Labor inspectors, should be able to decide issues such as where weapons will be stored and where suspects will be interviewed. Since the statute was inapplicable the suit failed. The Court contrasted the facts in this case to that of *Balsamo v. City of New York*,[43] in which an officer banged his knee on the sharp edge of a patrol units unpadded computer console while responding to an emergency call. Section 27-a would apply in this case because this was the type occupational injury the law was designed to avoid and did not arise "from risks unique to police work".

In *Gonzalez v. Iocoveillo & the City of New York*,[44] the court sustained a cause of action for a statutory violation. A police officer was injured when the police car she was riding in as "recorder" went through a red light and struck another vehicle. Plaintiff sued seeking recovery under the statutory cause of action provided for in GML §205-e, alleging the operator violated Vehicle and Traffic Law §1104. The trial court and the Appellate Division (First Dept.) upheld her claim. The City appealed to the Court of Appeals arguing that GML §205-e did not authorize fellow-officer law suits, i.e, action against a co-employee or employer, and that Vehicle and Traffic Law §1104 could not serve as a predicate for this kind of liability. The Court disagreed with the City's position and held that fellow-officer suits could be brought under GML §205-e, for cases involving New York City officers, and that Vehicle and Traffic Law §1104 could provide a basis for such action. The Court referred to the 1966 amendments to the statutes, which are discussed in the next section.

Firefighter's Rule Modified to Permit Some Law Suits

In 1996, the Legislature enacted new laws designed to "offer an umbrella of protection for police officers, who, in the course of their many and varied duties, are injured by the negligence of anyone who violates any relevant statute, ordinance, code, rule and/or regulation." (Legislative Intent, Section 1 of Laws of 1996, Chapter 703, effective October 9, 1966.)

One of the new laws is designed to expand the right of officers to sue third parties, other than their employer or co-employees, for common-law negligence. A new section was added to the General Obligations Law, §11-106, which reads as follows:

§11-106 Compensation for injury to police officers and firefighters or their estates.

1. In addition to any other right of action or recovery otherwise available under law, whenever any police officer or firefighter suffers any injury, disease or death while in the lawful discharge of his official duties and that injury, disease or death is proximately caused by the neglect, wilful omission or intentional, wilful or culpable conduct of any person or entity, **other than that police officer's or firefighter's employer or co-employee**, (emphasis added), the police officer or firefighter suffering that injury or disease, or in the case of death, a representative of that police officer or firefighter may seek recovery and damages from the person or entity whose neglect, wilful omission, or intentional, wilful, or culpable conduct resulted in that injury, disease or death.

2. Nothing in this section shall be deemed to expand or restrict the existing liability of an employer or co-employee at common law or under section two hundred five-a and two hundred five-e of the General Municipal Law for injuries or death sustained in the line of duty by any police officer or firefighter.

This new law expands the right of officers to bring negligence actions against third parties, except their employer or co-workers, which might have previously been barred by the firefighter's rule. For example, in *Sikes v. Reliance Federal Bank*[45] the court allowed a police officer to sue for injuries sustained when he fell down a flight of slippery stairs while responding to a false alarm. The stairs had recently been waxed by an employee of the building. These facts involve an action for common law negligence that prior to the enacting of

§11-106, and the amendment to §205-e discussed below, would have been prohibited by the "firefighter's rule." The previous section of law addressed common-law negligence actions. The legislation also expanded the right to bring actions under GML §205-e for breaches of statutes or regulations, etc.

GML. §205-e was amended by adding a new subdivision 3 to read as follows:

> This section shall be deemed to provide a right of action regardless of whether the injury or death is caused by the violation of a provision which codifies a common-law duty and regardless of whether the injury or death is caused by the violation of a provision prohibiting activities or conditions which increase the dangers inherent in the work of any officer, member, agent or employee of any police department.

GML §205-a, relating to firefighters, was also similarly amended.

As noted above in *Gonzalez,* the Court indicated that a GML §205-e action could be brought against a co-employee or employer. However it should be noted that these cases arise out of New York City where police and fire officers are not covered by the Workers' Compensation Law. For those employees covered by the Workers' Compensation Law the provisions in the law against suing an employer must also be considered.

New Constitutional Tort Created In New York

In the case of *Brown v. State of New York,*[46] the Court of Appeals created a new principle of law establishing that the Court of Claims has jurisdiction over claims against the state based upon violations of the New York

State Constitution and is not limited to common law tort causes of action. The court defined a **"constitutional tort"** as "any action for damages for violation of a constitutional right against a government or individual defendants."

The case arose from a bizarre set of facts. On September 4, 1992, in the City of Oneonta, an elderly white woman was attacked at knife point near the State University campus. She described her attacker as a black male, and the police determined he may have cut his hand during the attack. With no particular suspect in mind, the State Police, local police and SUCO security obtained a list of all African-American males attending the college. Each student was questioned and their hands and forearms were inspected. No suspect was discovered and then the police launched a five day "street sweep" in which every non-white male found in and around the City of Oneonta was stopped and questioned.

The petitioners brought a class action suit on behalf of the non-white males who were stopped. They argue that the conduct of the officers was racially motivated and the State of New York thus violated rights protected by the *Fourth* and *Fourteenth Amendments* of the United States Constitution, *Article 1 §11* and *§12* of the New York State Constitution and Article 4 §40-c of the New York Civil Rights Law. The petitioners also seek damages under 42 U.S.C §1981 for the negligent training and/or supervision of the officers.

Actions against the State of New York must be brought in the Court of Claims and that Court dismissed the claims holding that *constitutional torts* are not cognizable in that Court absent a link to a common law tort, that actions for negligent training and supervision are also not cognizable and that actions based on 42 U.S.C. §1981 cannot be brought against the state. The Appellate Division affirmed. The Court of Appeals reinstated the *constitutional tort* claims and the claims for negligent training and supervision. The court sustained the dismissal of the §1981 claim.

This holding greatly expands the potential vicarious liability of the state for the actions of its police agents. It offers substantially broader protections under the New York Constitution then are available under the United States Constitution.[47] It remains to be seen if dissenting Judge Bellacosa's qualms about the holding opening up the doors to a flood of lawsuits are realized. The Court of Appeals did, however, emphasize the limitations of the *Brown* decision in *Martinez v. Schenectady*.[48] In that case Martinez was convicted of drug charges and spent four years in prison. After an appeal the Court of Appeals determined that there had been insufficient information in the original warrant application to support its issuance and Martinez was released from prison. She sought money damages in her subsequent lawsuit. The Court emphasized the *Brown* decision was not applicable to these facts. No one was arrested in *Brown* so no relief was available to the plaintiff's besides monetary damages. For *Brown* to apply claimants must establish their rights were violated and sufficient grounds to show they are entitled to damages. Here, Martinez was granted suppression of evidence and a reversal of her conviction due to a technical error. In *Brown* monetary damages was the only means of deterring subsequent police actions of that nature. In *Martinez* type cases the suppression of evidence and reversal of a conviction has sufficient deterrent value.

Part III
FEDERAL CIVIL RIGHTS ACTIONS

What is a "Section 1983" action?

The term refers to a civil proceeding authorized under Section 1983 of Title 42 of the United States Code. The statute reads in part:

> Every person who, under color of any statute, ordinance, regulation, custom or usage, of any State or Territory, subjects, or causes to be subjected any citizen of the United States or other persons within the jurisdiction thereof to the deprivation of any rights, privileges, or immunities secured by the Constitution and laws, shall be liable to the party injured in an action at law, suit in equity, or other proper proceeding for redress.

This law, originally adopted in 1871, has in recent years become the basis of a variety of law suits against police officers, correction officers, parole and probation officers, and others who act "under color of law."

What are the elements of a "Section 1983" action?

There are four elements which must be present in an action:

(i) the defendant must be a natural person or a local government
(ii) the defendant must be acting "under color of law."
(iii) the violation must be of a federal constitutional or federally protected right
(iv) the violation must reach a constitutional level. A slight push or touching would not rise to a constitutional level,[49] but a brief detention could.[50]

When is an officer "acting under color of law?"

"Acting under color of law" means using powers given through state law and made possible only because the officer is clothed with the authority of the state. An officer can be acting under color of law even when there is an abuse of power. For example, an officer unlawfully beats a person in his custody; the action is not authorized but courts would find that the officer was acting under color of law.

Off-duty situations present a difficult problem. Each case has to be evaluated to determine if there is liability. In *Bonsignore v. City of New York*,[51] it was held that an off-duty police officer who shot his wife with his revolver and then shot himself was not acting under color of law. In another case, an officer "moonlighting" as a private security officer made an arrest after identifying himself as a police officer and processed the arrest at the station house. He was found to be acting under color of law.[52]

What are some of the constitutional rights that are commonly used as the basis of a "Section 1983" action?

Some of the areas that can give rise to actionable conduct under federal civil rights law are:

False Arrest	Malicious Prosecution
Excessive Force	Deadly Force
Search & Seizure	Privacy
Free Speech	Self Incrimination
Right to Counsel	Denial of Medical Attention
Jail Suicides	Denial of Due Process

Can supervisors be held liable for the actions of a subordinate?

A supervisor is not liable for the actions of a subordinate under the doctrine of respondeat superior as in state court. However, certain conditions can arise that may lead to the individual liability of a supervisor. Some of them are:

>Participation in the unlawful act
>Failure to prevent the unlawful act
>Directing the unlawful act
>Ratifying the act after the fact

Liability may also arise if the plaintiff can establish that the supervisor was grossly negligent or acted with "deliberate indifference" to the rights of others in his/her failure to adequately supervise subordinates.[53] "..'Deliberate indifference' describes a mental state more blameworthy than negligence; but a plaintiff is not required to show that the defendant acted for the 'very purpose of causing harm or with knowledge that harm will result.' "[54] In other words, "deliberate indifference" does not rise to the level of intent but rather is more akin to recklessness. Areas of concern include:

Failure to train   Failure to supervise
Negligent hiring   Negligent retention
Negligent assignment   Negligent failure to supervise
          Negligent failure to discipline

All of these potential causes of action have a common theme: they involve the failure of a supervisor(s) to act when they should or failed to recognize when action would be necessary. When this theme of "supervisor liability" is discussed it is not limited to first line supervisors although they are in the forefront.[55] These principals of liability could potentially affect all levels of supervision right up to the chief law enforcement officer.[56]

The Second Circuit Court of Appeals has held that "the liability of a supervisor under §1983 can be shown in one or more of the following ways: (1) actual direct participation in the constitutional violation, (2) failure to remedy a wrong after being informed through a report or appeal, (3) creation of a policy or custom that sanctioned conduct amounting to a constitutional violation, or allowing such a policy or custom to continue, (4) grossly negligent supervision of subordinates who committed a violation, or (5) failure to act on information indicating that unconstitutional acts were occurring."[57]

Although the various courts interpret this area somewhat differently, there are some very basic rules that law enforcement supervisors of all ranks should follow to manage potential liability. The first is to do a complete, thorough background investigation on all new hires and disqualify those who deserve to be. Second, develop comprehensive policies regarding discipline and investigations into breaches of discipline. The third would be to enforce those policies and **thoroughly investigate and document all complaints,** whether internal (i.e. supervisor spots a transgression) or external (i.e. citizen complaint). Being able to produce thorough documentation of discipline can prevent a finding of "deliberate indifference". Fourth, agencies should employ some type of early warning system to track things like incidents involving use of force and officer complaints. Finally supervisors must remember that if they see it or hear it, they must write it. The simple act of documentation can help to avoid supervisor liability. In *Shaw v. Stroud*[58] a North Carolina State Trooper, Morris, shot and killed a vehicle driver during a struggle that developed after a traffic stop. Morris was a seven year veteran and for his first five years he was supervised by Sgt. Stroud. During this time period Stroud apparently ignored, and also seemingly found humorous, numerous complaints against Morris regarding excessive use of force. Sgt. Smith took over as Morris's supervisor for the 15 month period leading up to the shooting. During the transition Stroud never told Smith about any prior complaints against Morris. Nevertheless Morris still was generating force complaints that Smith then acted upon. Along with closely monitoring Morris's actions Smith rode several shifts with him. He also kept his supervisors apprised of these complaints. After the shooting, the wife of the driver commenced an action that included Morris, Stroud and Smith. Upon motion for summary judgment the district court found that Stroud actions amounted to deliberate indifference while Smith's did not. Therefore Smith was removed from the action while Stroud would have to defend his behavior at trial. The Court of Appeals affirmed this holding. Stroud more than likely does not find Morris's actions humorous anymore.

Can a municipality be held liable under Section 1983?

In *Monell v. Dept. of Social Services*,[59] the U.S. Supreme Court held that municipalities could be liable when an "official policy" of the municipality is the cause of unconstitutional actions taken by employees. Although many cases have been brought under this theory, there is no clear cut definition of what constitutes "official policy." Cases have been brought which include allegations concerning inadequate training, condoning illegal searches, assaults, mistreatment of prisoners, harassment of individuals or groups, a policy of inadequate supervision or discipline and many other theories.

Liability for the failure to train requires a showing of *deliberate indifference* by the municipality to the rights of persons who deal with the police.

How can an agency be held liable for "failure to train"?

In the *City of Canton v. Harris*[60] the United States Supreme Court held that "the inadequacy of police training may serve as the basis for §1983 liability only where the failure to train amounts to deliberate indifference to the rights of persons with whom the police come into contact."[61] The Court further stated that "for liability to attach in this circumstance the identified deficiency in a city's training program must be closely related to the ultimate injury."[62]

The *Canton* holding, and those decisions that have followed, require that law enforcement agencies perform a continual job analysis. If any given police task is identified as one that is a usual and recurring one that officers must deal with then they must be adequately trained in that task. While all foreseeable aspects of policing should be covered in a comprehensive training program, reality dictates that priorities need to be designated. For example, it is certainly a fair statement that officers will constantly have to apply the laws regarding search and seizure. Therefore agencies must have continual training programs focusing on the specific areas of law most likely to be encountered on a recurring basis. Any job analysis should also prioritize areas of performance based upon whether the task is one of high risk or low risk and how frequently the task may be faced by officers. An example of a task that is high risk and also occurs at a high frequency would be emergency vehicle operations. Under the holding of *Canton*, therefore, agencies should have comprehensive policies on emergency response and train on them regularly. The use of deadly physical force is an example of a task that is high risk but low frequency. Nevertheless due to the "high risk" designation it too must be the subject of constant, comprehensive training and policy as these are the types of tasks that when performed incorrectly will land the agency in court. High risk tasks should be the subject of the most training while the low risk, low frequency tasks, while still important, may not have to be revisited as often. Documentation of all training is absolutely crucial. Without it the training never occurred.

What are the defenses of "absolute immunity" and "qualified immunity?"

The defense of absolute immunity means that there is no liability at all for actions taken in an official capacity. This defense is generally limited to judges, prosecutors and legislators. There is one instance when police officers enjoy absolute immunity from civil liability and that is when they are testifying in a trial, even if such testimony is perjurious.[63]

Police officers may be entitled to qualified immunity in a Section 1983 action. Qualified immunity assures law enforcement officers that they "will not be held personally liable as long as their actions are reasonable in light of current American law."[64] Qualified immunity is meant to protect responsible law enforcement officers "from undue interference with their duties and from the potentially disabling threat of liability. It protects "all but the plainly incompetent or those who knowingly violate the law."[65] When determining whether qualified immunity is appropriate in a particular case two questions must be answered. The first is whether the officers' conduct violated a constitutional right. If not no further inquiry is necessary. If the answer is yes then the second question is whether that right was clearly established.[66] The qualified immunity defense, therefore, is available to an officer who can establish that he/she acted with "objective legal reasonableness," that is, a reasonably well trained officer would not have known the conduct would violate claimant's constitutional rights. The recent case of *Vives v. City of New York*,[67] involves this complicated issue and is worth reviewing. Vives was a 66 year old man who sent non-threatening religious and political materials to a candidate for Lieutenant Governor. His stated intent was to alarm her, as well as the thousands of other people he also sent the material to, about certain world events. The material was generic and not personalized to the candidate. He was arrested for aggravated harassment, Penal Law §240.30(1), by two detectives. The district attorneys office declined to prosecute the case however, and he was released on the same day. Vives then brought suit against the officers and the city, claiming his First and Fourth Amendment rights were violated.

The District Court denied the detective's motion for summary judgment in regards to qualified immunity and held that the language of the statute that prohibited communications intended to annoy or alarm was unconstitutional. The Court reviewed a number of cases that questioned the constitutionality of the sections and felt that it should have been clear that the applicable statute was unconstitutional, even though none of the cases reviewed clearly held it to be so. The Second Circuit Court of Appeals reversed this decision. The Appellate Court disagreed with the District Courts interpretation of the prior cases and found that it was appropriate for the detectives to rely on the "presumptive constitutionality of section 240.30(1)"[68] The case was sent back to the District Court to enter judgment in favor of the detectives. This meant the suit could still proceed as against the city and any other pending issues, but the individual officers will not have any personal liability. The Second Circuit also failed to decide the issue as to whether §240.30(1) is constitutional or not, leaving this issue still up in the air.

On remand, therefore, the District Court once again reaffirmed its holding that the statute was unconstitutional and held the city to be liable.[69] This will likely be appealed by the City and will once again be before the Second Circuit.

It is important to understand that if there had been a prior case finding that section of law unconstitutional, and it was still enforced, qualified immunity would not apply and personal liability would be likely. This would be true whether the officers actually knew that the section had been held unconstitutional. This point highlights the importance of departments to have ongoing legal update training.

The legal issues concerning qualified immunity are many and complex; an excellent summary can be found in *Personal Liability: The Qualified Immunity Defense*, Daniel L. Schofield, F.B.I. Bulletin, March, 1990. See **"Can Ride-along situations Violate the Fourth Amendment?"** in section below.

Can "Ride-along" situations violate the Fourth Amendment?

In *Wilson v. Lane, et al.*[70] Federal Marshals and local County police officers had arrest warrants for one Dominic Wilson. The team of officers, *accompanied by a reporter and a photographer from the Washington Post*, entered the home of Wilson's parents at 6:45 a.m. Mr. & Mrs. Wilson were still in bed, and Mr. Wilson, clad only in briefs, ran into the living room and confronted the police. He was subdued on the floor. The photographer took several pictures, including one of Mr. Wilson lying on the floor with an officer's knee in his back and a gun to his head. Mrs. Wilson, clad only in a night gown, witnessed her husband plight. The son was not found in the premises and the officers left. The Washington Post did not publish any of the pictures. Both police agencies had policies that authorized the presence of reporters when executing warrants.

The Wilsons sued the officers for violating their Fourth Amendment rights. The officers pleaded the defense of qualified immunity, the District Court rejected the defense but the Circuit Court of Appeals upheld the defense. It found that no court had held (at the time of the search) that media presence during a police entry into a premise was a violation of the Fourth Amendment and thus no "clearly established" right was violated. The Court of Appeals did not rule on the issue of whether the police violated the Fourth Amendment. However, the U.S. Supreme Court unanimously found that "...such a "media ride along" does violate the Fourth Amendment..." but a majority found that "because the state of the law was not clearly established at the time the search in this case took place, the officers were entitled to the defense of qualified immunity." The Wilsons won on principle, but did not recover damages. Any officer who subsequently allows such a "media ride along" as in this case will not be entitled to qualified immunity as the constitutional rule is now "clear".

Can an officer be prosecuted for criminal acts for violating a person's civil rights?

Yes. The United States Department of Justice is empowered to prosecute public officials for the willful violation of federal civil rights under the provisions of Title 18 U.S.C §§241 and 242.

18 U.S.C. §242 makes it a crime, punishable by fine or imprisonment, for any person acting under color of law to **willfully** subject an inhabitant of the United States to the deprivation of federal constitutional or statutory rights. The prosecutor must prove a **willful intent** to deprive the victim of his/her rights.

18 U.S.C. §241 is a federal conspiracy statute. which provides for a fine or imprisonment, or both, if two or more persons conspire to deprive any citizen of the free exercise of a federal constitutional or statutory right. This section can be used against private persons as well as public officials.

These laws have been utilized against New York law enforcement officers. In 1988, two officers of the New York City Transit Police Department were convicted and imprisoned under §§241 and 242 for filing false charges against several male riders of the subway.[71] In Westchester County, a local officer was convicted of violating the rights of several women whom he unlawfully detained after stopping them for alleged traffic violations late at night on a deserted stretch of highway. He was sentenced to six consecutive one year terms of imprisonment.[72]

In these cases there were no State criminal charges filed. However, even if State criminal charges were brought and the officer was acquitted, the Justice Department can still bring criminal charges for the violation of civil rights. (See discussion of the *Livoti* case at page 24 (see endnote #31 Baez case). The federal prosecution does not violate the "double jeopardy" provisions of the Constitution.

NOTES

Endnotes

1. *Soarinen v. Ker and Village of Messina*, 84 N.Y.2d 494 (1995).

2. *Palella v. State of New York*, 141 A.D.2d 999 (1988)); *Campbell v. City of Elmira*, 84 N.Y.2d 505 (1995).

3. 35 A.D.2d 545, affmd.. 30 N.Y.2d 524 (1972); see also *Soarinen* and *Campbell* cases above.

4. *County of Sacramento, et al. v. Teri Lewis,* 523 US 833 (1998)

5. *Brower v. Inyo County*, 109 S.Ct 1378, (1989)

6. 109 S.Ct 1865, (1989).

7. *McCummings v. NYC Transit Authority*, 81 N.Y.2 d. 923.

8. 471 US 1 (1985).

9. *Papa v. City of New York*, 194 A.D.2d 527

10. *Ostrover v. City of New York*, 192 A.D.2d 115; 600 N.Y.S.2d 243 (1993)

11. *Maxwell v. City of New York*, 156 A.D.2d 28, (1990).

12. *Morillo v. City of New York, et al., 1997 U.S. Dist. Lexis 1665*, 1997 WL 72155 *3 (S.D.N.Y. Feb. 20, 1996) see also *Brawer v. Carter*, 937 F.Supp. 1071 (S.D.N.Y. 1996) (false arrest).

13. 69 N.Y.2d 255 (1987).

14. 14. 65 N.Y.2d 461 (1985).

15. 91 N.Y.2d 198 (1997)

16. 74 N.Y.2d 251 (1989).See also, *Kovit v. Estate of Hallums*, 4 N.Y.3d 499 (2005) (no special relationship established with plaintiff when officer told an upset woman at an accident scene to pull her car forward out of intersection and instead backed up into plaintiff. No direct contact with plaintiff established) and *Lazan v. County of Suffolk*, same cite as Hallums (plaintiff had pulled over to the side of the road as he was "not feeling well." Officer told him to drive to closest gas station and he hit a guardrail, sustaining serious injuries. No special relationship established as officer could not have known under these circumstances this would lead to harm).

17. *Berliner v. Thompson*, 174 A.D.2d 220 (3rd Dept. 1992) discussing the holding of *Sorichetti v. City of New York*, 65 N.Y.2d 461 (1985).

18. 125 S.Ct. 2796 (2005).

19. *Merced v. City of New York*, 75 N.Y.2d 798 (1990)). See also, *Greene v. City of New York*, S.Ct. Queens, 588 N.Y.S.2d 98 (1992).

20. *DeLong* v. *County of Erie*; 60 N.Y.2d 296, (1983).

21. *Parvi v. City of Kingston, 41 N.Y.2d* 553, 559.

22. *Thomas Walsh, as Admin.. v. Town of Cheektowaga*, 237 A.D.2d 947 (4th Dept. 1997).

23. 217 A.D.2d 934, see also *Stata v. Village of Waterford, 225 A.D.2d 163, 649 N.Y.S.2d 232*, concerning failure of firefighters to take steps to rescue victim of a fire.

24. *Evers v. Westerberg*, 32 N.Y.2d 684 (1973); *Crosby v. Town of Bethlehem*, 90 A.D.2d 134 (1982).

25. 181 A.D.2d 233 (1992); see *Young v. Koch*, 128 Misc.2d 119, (1985).

26. 173 A.D.2d 276 (1st Dept. 1991).

27. 188 A.D.2d 313 (1st Dept. 1992).

28. 187 A.D.2d 946, affmd.. 83 N.Y.2d 141 (1994).

29. 98 A.D.2d 529 (1984).

30. See also *Alifieris v. American Air Lines*, 63 N.Y.2d 370 (1986) and *Becker v. City of New York*, 192 Misc.2d 194 (NYC Ct. Kings Co. 2002).

31. *Baez v. City of New York;* Supreme Court, Bronx, McKeon, J.; NYLJ, August 27, 1998

32. *Cepeda v. Coughlin*, 128 A.D.2d 995 (1987), appeal denied, 70 N.Y.2d 602.

33. *Hartford Acc. & Indem. Co. v. Village of Hempstead*, 48 N.Y.2d 218 (1979); *The Home Insurance Co. v. American Home Products Co.*, 75 N.Y.2d 196 (1990).

34. *Hartford* case, Note 31, supra

35. 376 U.S. 254 (1964),

36. *Santangelo v. State*, 71 N.Y.2d 393, at 397 (1988).

37. *Ciervo v. City of New York*, 93 N.Y.2d 465 (1999).

38. *Cooper v. City of New York*, 81 N.Y.2d 584, *Ruotolo v. State*, 83 N.Y.2d 255, *Desmond v. City of New York*, 88 N.Y.2d 464.

39. *Williams v. City of New York*, 2 N.Y.3d 352 (2004).

40. *Williams*, supra at 364. See also *Galapo v. City of New York*, 95 N.Y.2d 568 (2000) and *Desmond v. City of New York*, 88 N.Y.2d 455 (1996).

41. See *Galapo* and *Desmond*, in previous endnote.

42. 2 N.Y.3d 352 (2004).

43. 287 A.D.2d 22 (2d Dept. 2001).

44. 93 N.Y.2d 539; 999.

45. 234 A.D.2d 446, (2nd Dept. 1996).

46. 89 N.Y.2d 172 (1996).

47. *Monell v. N.Y.C. Department of Social Services*, 436 U.S. 658; *Bivens v. Six Unknown Agents of Federal Bureau of Narcotics*, 403 U.S. 388.

48. 97 N.Y.2d 78 (2001).

49. *Hudson v. McMillan*, 503 U.S.1 (1992).

50. *U.S. v. Langer*, 958 F2d 522, (2 Cir. 1992)

51. 683 F2d 635 (2Cir.1982).

52. *Lusby v. TG&Y Stores*, 749 F2d 1423 (10 Cir. 1984, *vacated in* 474 U.S. 805, *re-aff'd on remand* 796 F.2d 1307 (10 Cir.1984).

53. *City of Canton v. Harris*, 489 U.S. 378 (1989).

54. *Hernandez v. Keane*, 341 F.3d 137, 144 (2nd Cir. 2003), quoting *Farmer v. Brennan*, 511 U.S. 825, 835 (1994).

55. See *Baker v. Monroe Township*, 50 F.3d 1186 (3rd Cir. 1995) and *Gutierrez-Rodriguez v. Cartagena, et al.*, 882 F.2d 553 (1st Cir. 1989).

56. *Larez v. City of Los Angeles, et al.*, 946 F.2d 630 (9th Cir. 1991).

57. *Hernandez v. Keane*, 341 F.3d 137, 145 (2nd Cir. 2003).

58. *Shaw v. Stroud*, 13 F.3d 791 (4th Cir. 1994).

59. 436 U.S. 658 (1978).

60. *City of Canton v. Harris*, 489 U.S. 378 (1989).

61. *Id*, at 388.

62. *Id*, at 391.

63. *Briscoe v. LaHue*, 460 U.S. 325 (1983)). See *White v. Frank and City of Poughkeepsie*, 855 F2d 956 (1988) concerning false testimony by a police officer before a Grand Jury.

64. *Anderson v. Creighton*, 483 U.S. 635 (1987).-

65. *Malley v. Briggs*, 475 U.S. 335 (1986).

66. *Saucier v. Katz*, 533 U.S. 194 (2001).

67. 405 F.3d 115 (2nd Circuit 2005).

68. *Id*. at p. 118.

69. *Vives v. City of New York,* 2004 WL2997947 (SDNY, Dec. 27, 2004)

70. 526 U.S. 603, (1999). See also *Hanlon v. Berger,* 526 U.S. 808 (1999) decided the same time as *Wilson.*

71. *U.S. v. McDermott*, 918 F.2d. 319 (2nd Cir. 1990), *cert. denied* 500 U.S. 904 (1991).

72. *U.S. v. Langer*, 958 F.2d 522 (2nd Cir. 1992).

Index

Acting under color of law 36
Assault and battery 10
Balsamo v. City of New York 29
Bonsignore v. City of New York 36
Brown v. State of New York 32
City of Canton v. Harris 40
Constitutional tort 33
Cuffy v. City of New York 13
Damages; compensatory
    defined 2
Damages; nominal
    defined 2
Damages; punitive 26
    defined 2
Deadly physical force 8
Deliberate indifference 37-40
Desa v. City of N.Y. 23
Emergency vehicle operation 4
Failure to train 40
False arrest 11
Firefighter's rule 27, 28, 30-32
Gonzalez v. Iocoveillo & the City of New York 29
Graham v. Connor 7
Immunity, defenses of
    absolute / qualified 41
Indemnification 5
    defined 2
    laws relating to 20
    of Corrections employees 25
    punitive damages 26
Intentional torts 10
Joseph v. City of Buffalo 23
Kircher v. City of Jamestown 16
Malicious prosecution 12
Martinez v. Schenectady 34
Mastroianni v. County of Suffolk 15
McCormick v. City of New York 28
Monell v. Dept. of Social Services 39
Municipal employees 20
Negligence
    defined 1

Polak v. City of Schenectady 21
Reckless disregard standard 4
Respondeat superior
    defined 2
Ride-along situations 43
Roadblock, establishment 6
Section 1983 action 35
    constitutional rights 36
    elements of 35
Shaw v. Stroud 38
Shocks the conscience standard 5
Sikes v. Reliance Federal Bank 31
Sorichetti v. City of New York 14
Special relationship 13
State employees 20
Stavitz v. City of N.Y. 23
Sullivan v. New York Times 27
Supervisor liability
    Federal law 37
    State law 2
Tennessee v. Garner 8
Thain v. City of New York 4
Thomas v. City of Auburn 19
Tort
    defined 1
Tort; constitutional
    defined 1
Tort; intentional
    defined 1
Town of Castle Rock, Colorado v. Gonzales 17
Use of force; standards 6
Vives v. City of New York 42
Williams v. City of New York 28
Wilson v. City of N.Y. 22
Wilson v. Lane 43
Wrongful conduct
    consequences 3

NOTES

NOTES

Other Titles of Interest from Looseleaf Law Publications, Inc.

Building a Successful Law Enforcement Career
Common Sense Wisdom for the New Officer
by Lt. Ryan E. Melsky

Anatomy of a Motor Vehicle Stop
Essentials of Safe Traffic Enforcement
by Joseph & Matthew Petrocelli

Advanced Vehicle Stop Tactics
Skills for Today's Survival Conscious Officer
by Michael T. Rayburn

Advanced Patrol Tactics
Skills for Today's Street Cop
by Michael T. Rayburn

How to Really, *Really* Write Those Boring Police Reports
by Kimberly Clark

Deadly Force
Constitutional Standards, Federal Guidelines and Officer Survival
by John Michael Callahan, Jr.

Use of Force
Expert Guidance for Decisive Force Response
by Brian A. Kinnaird

Handgun Combatives
by Dave Spaulding

Essential Guide to Handguns for Personal Defense and Protection
by Steven R. Rementer and Bruce M. Eimer, Ph.D.

Suicide by Cop
*Practical Direction for Recognition,
Resolution and Recovery*
by Vivian Lord

Police Sergeant Examination Preparation Guide
by Larry Jetmore

Path of the Warrior
*An Ethical Guide to Personal &
Professional Development in the Field of
Criminal Justice*
by Larry F. Jetmore

The COMPSTAT Paradigm
*Management Accountability in Policing,
Business and the Public Sector*
by Vincent E. Henry, CPP, Ph.D.

The New Age of Police Supervision and Management
A Behavioral Concept
by Michael A. Petrillo & Daniel R. DelBagno

Effective Police Leadership - 2nd Edition
Moving Beyond Management
by Thomas E. Baker, Lt. Col. MP USAR (Ret.)

The Lou Savelli Pocketguides -

Gangs Across America and Their Symbols
Identity Theft - Understanding and Investigation
Guide for the War on Terror
Basic Crime Scene Investigation

---

*FOR AN UP-TO-DATE LIST OF ALL OF OUR PUBLICATIONS,
PLEASE CALL US FOR A CATALOG OR CHECK OUR WEBSITE.*

(800) 647-5547   www.LooseleafLaw.com